NATIONAL GEOGRAPHIC

T0045500

What Shapes Do You See?

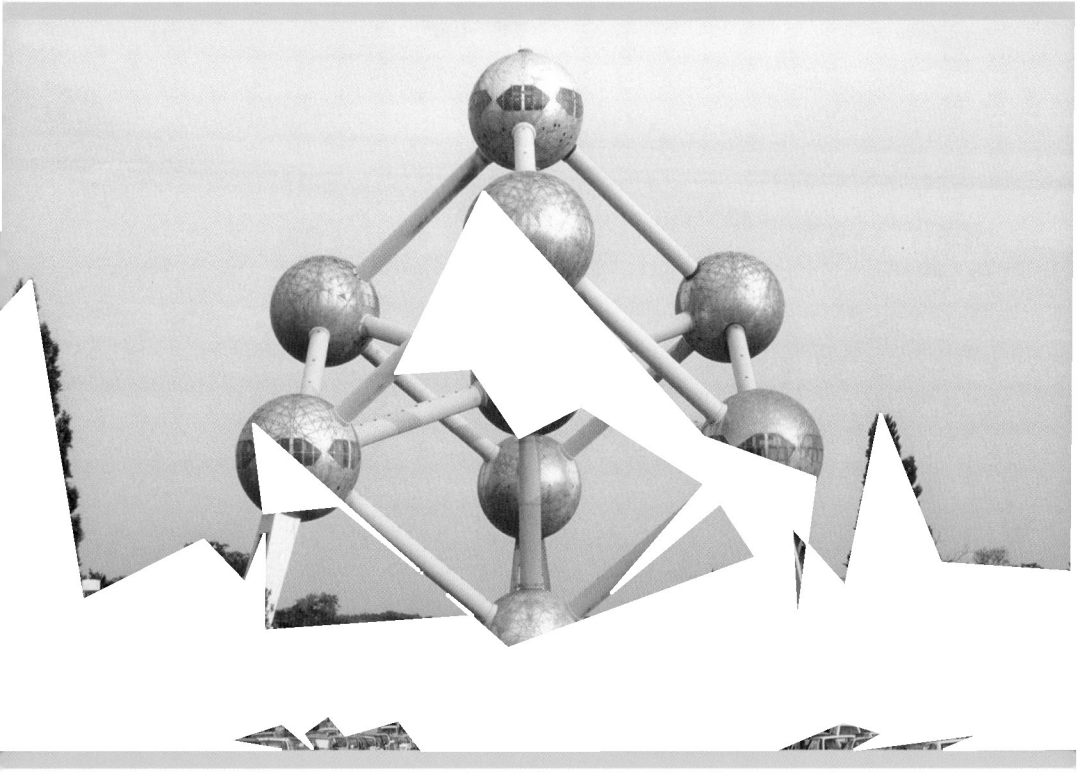

Matthew Taylor

cube

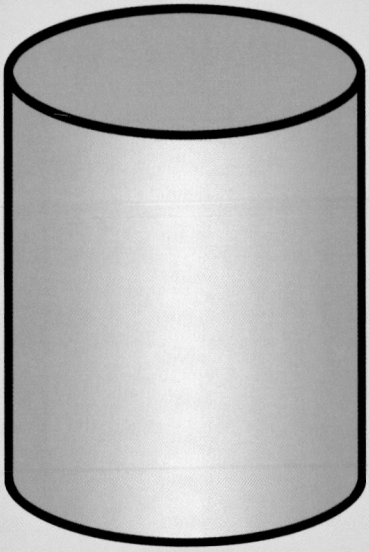

cylinder

pyramid

sphere

What shape do you see?

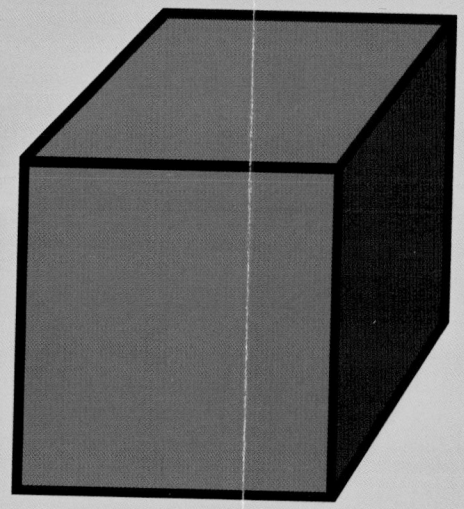

cube

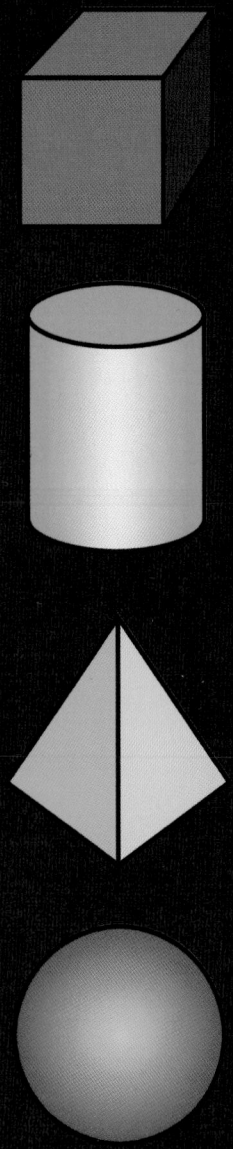

Lift the flap.

What shape do you see?

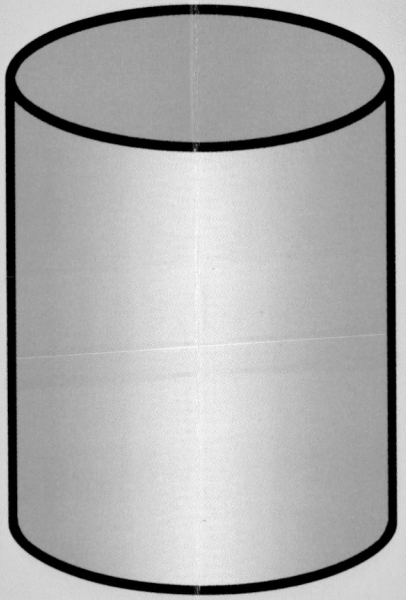

cylinder

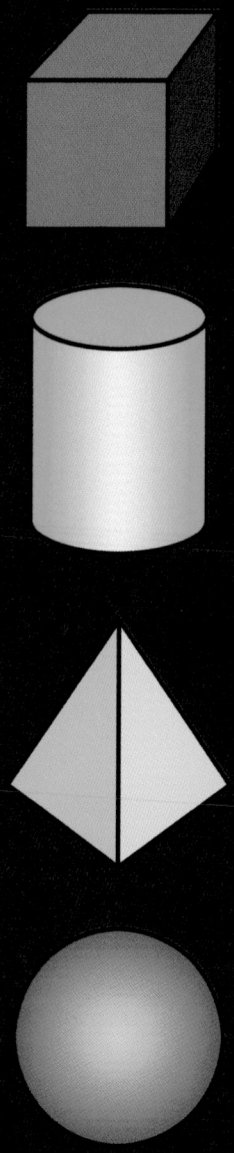

Lift the flap.

What shape do you see?

pyramid

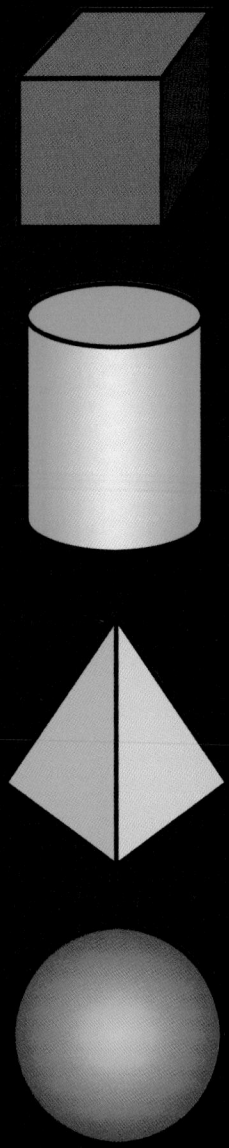

Lift the flap.

What shape do you see?

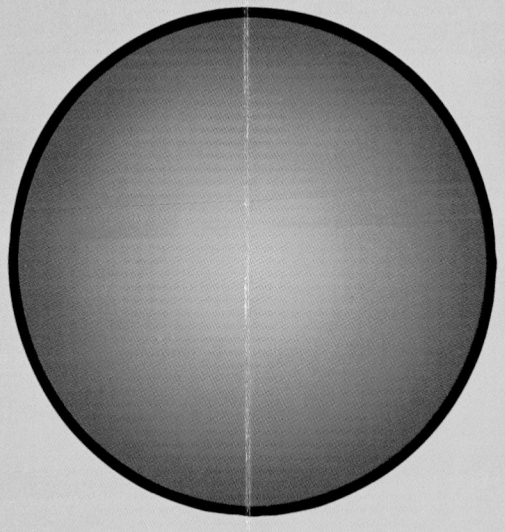

sphere

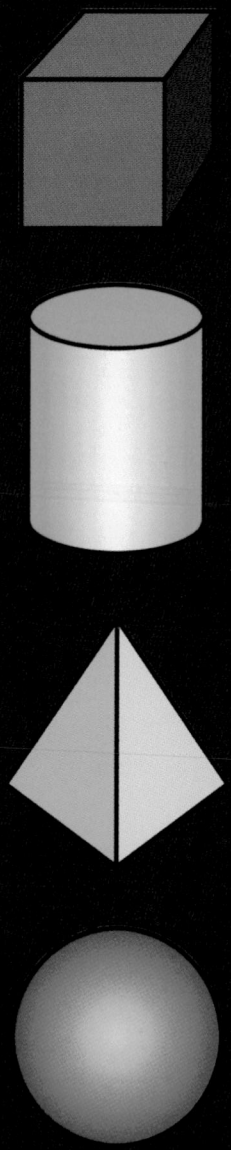

Lift the flap.

Picture Glossary

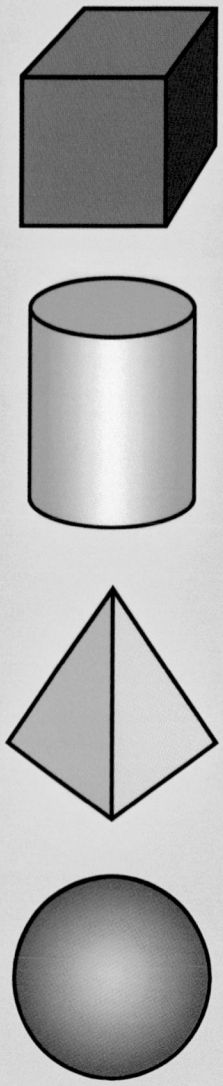

cube

cylinder

pyramid

sphere